SUGAR SKULLS

ADULT COLORING BOOK

SUGAR SKULLS (ADULT COLORING BOOK)
By
Various Artist
Copyright © Various Artist 2017
Cover Copyright © Ravenswood Publishing 2017
Published by Chimera
(An Imprint of Ravenswood Publishing)

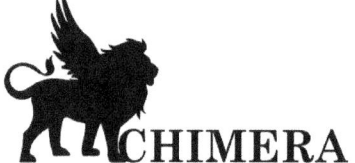
CHIMERA

All illustrations within are compiled works of various artists. Ravenswood makes no claim to any of the art inside this book. All royalties go to charity.

Ravenswood Publishing
http://www.ravenswoodpublishing.com

Paperback orders can be made through Createspace
http://www.createspace.com

Printed in the United States of American
First Edition
10 9 8 7 6 5 4 3 2 1

ISBN-13: 978-1977994714
ISBN-10: 1977994717

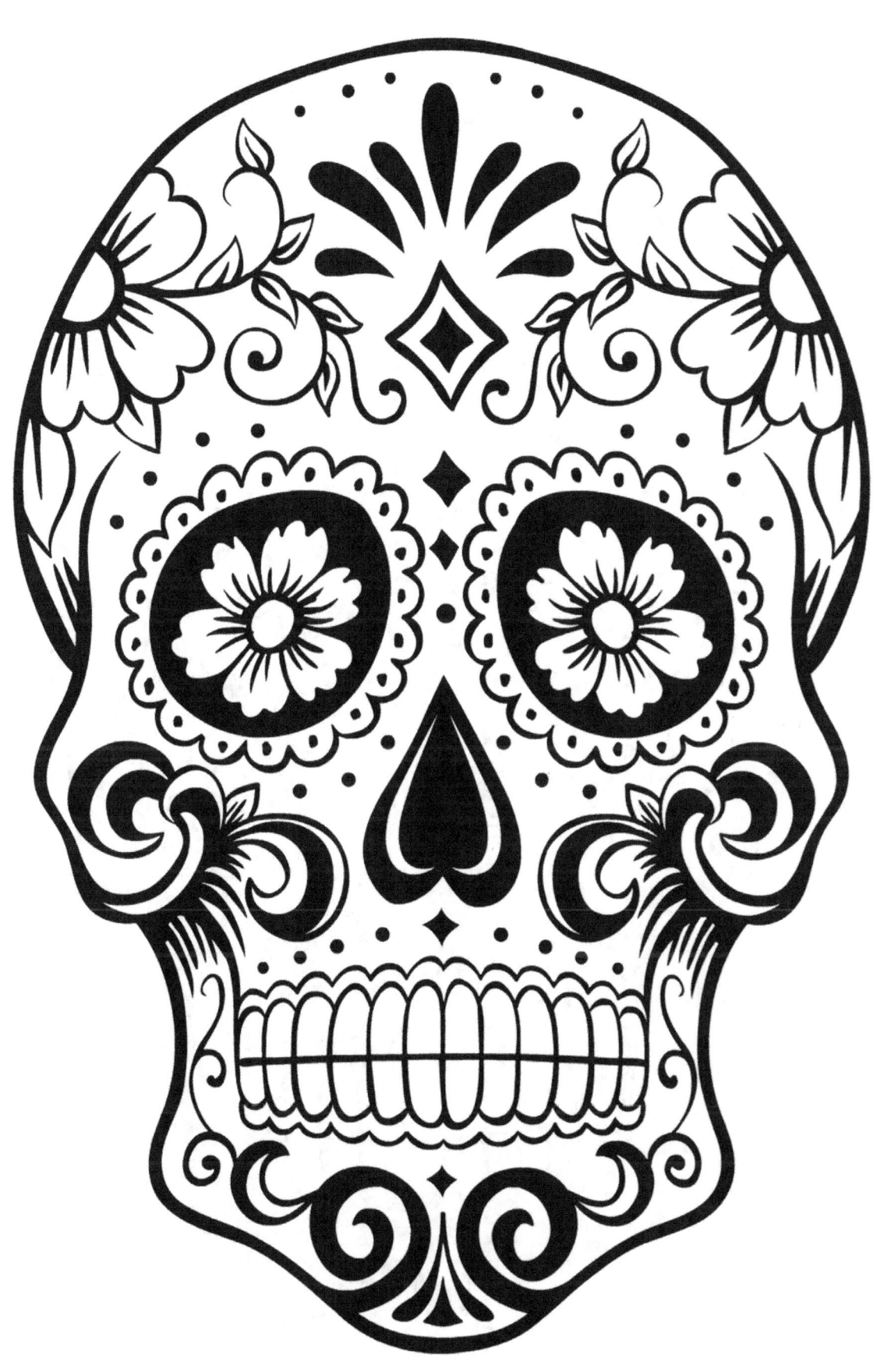

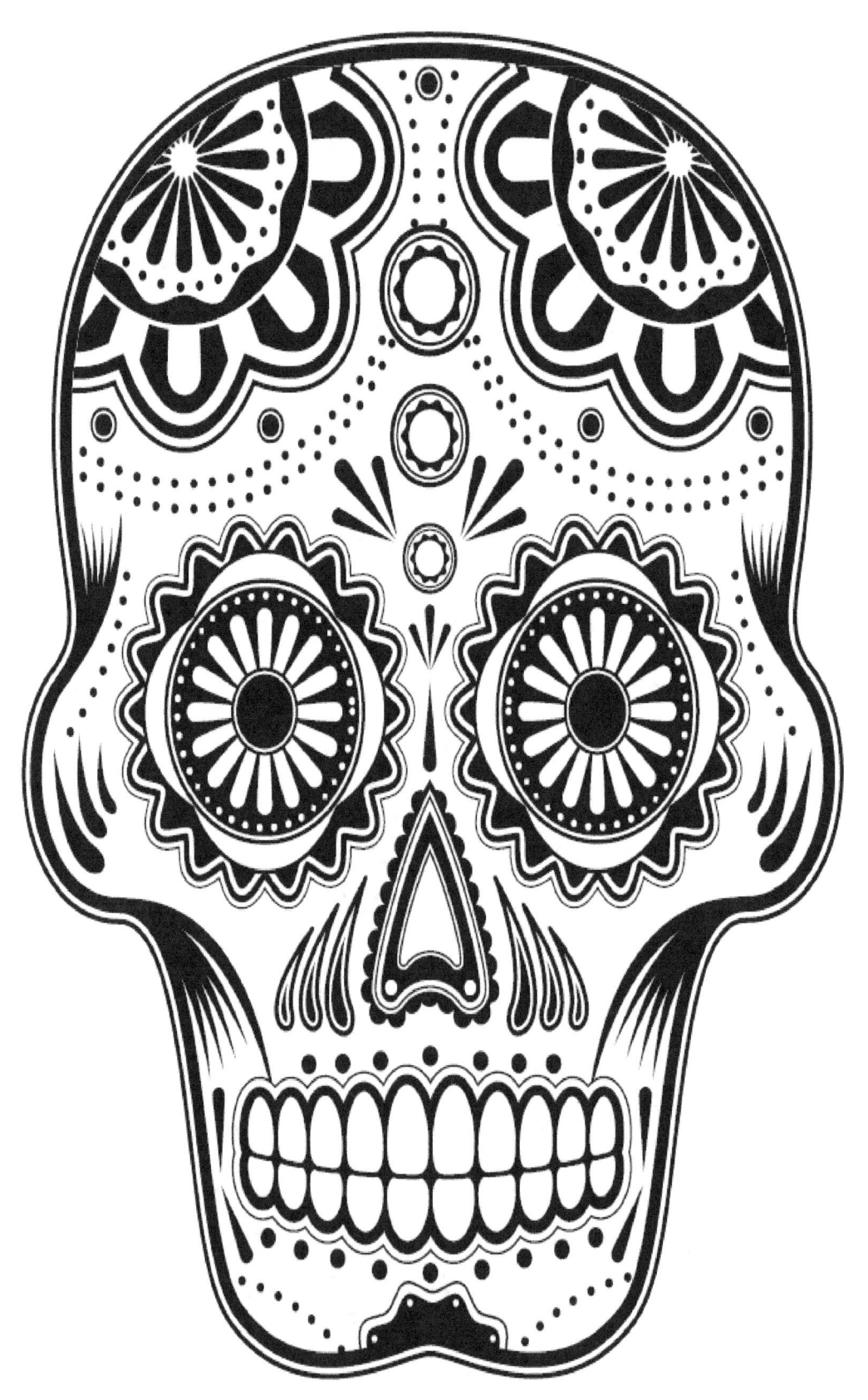

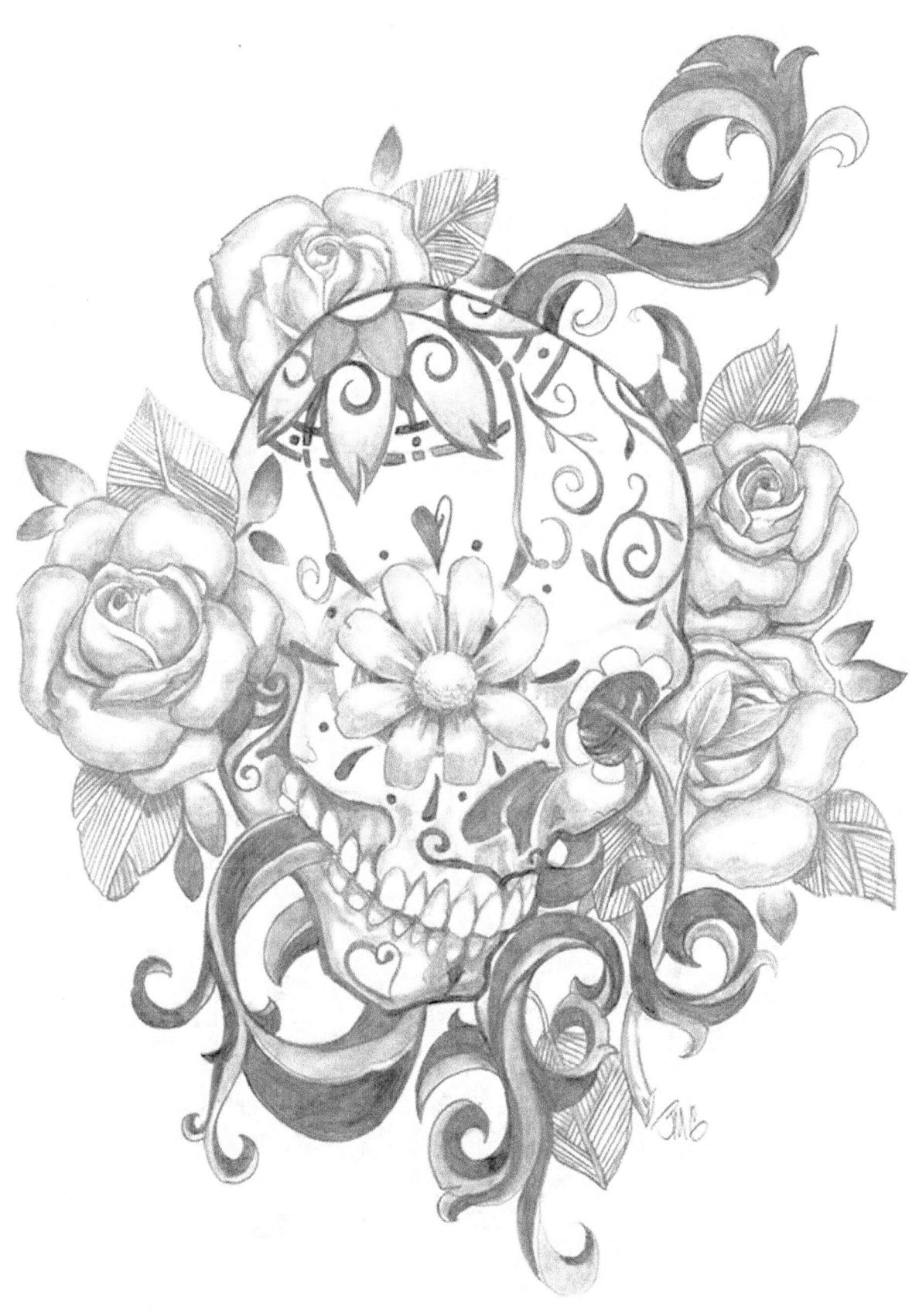

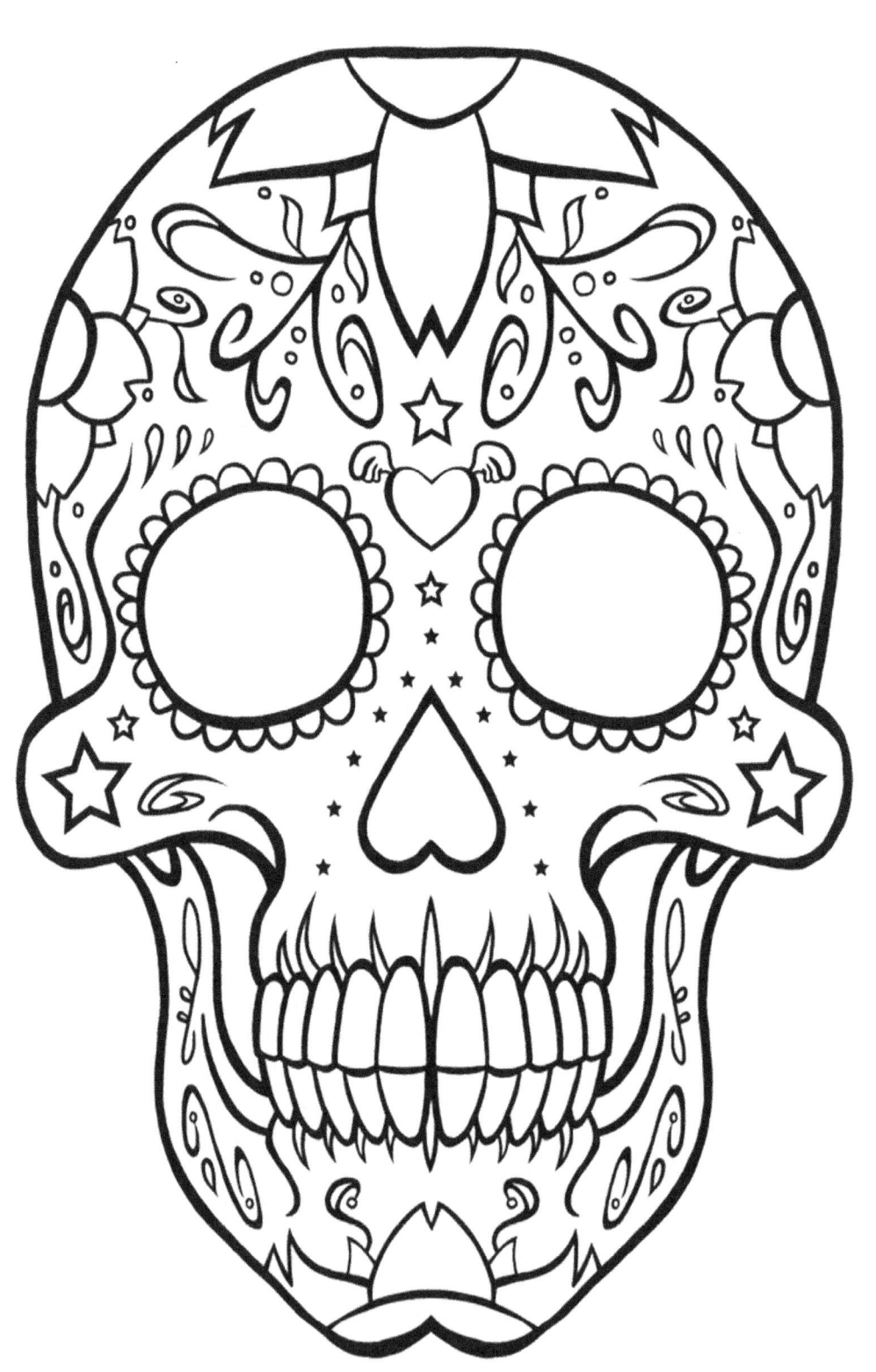

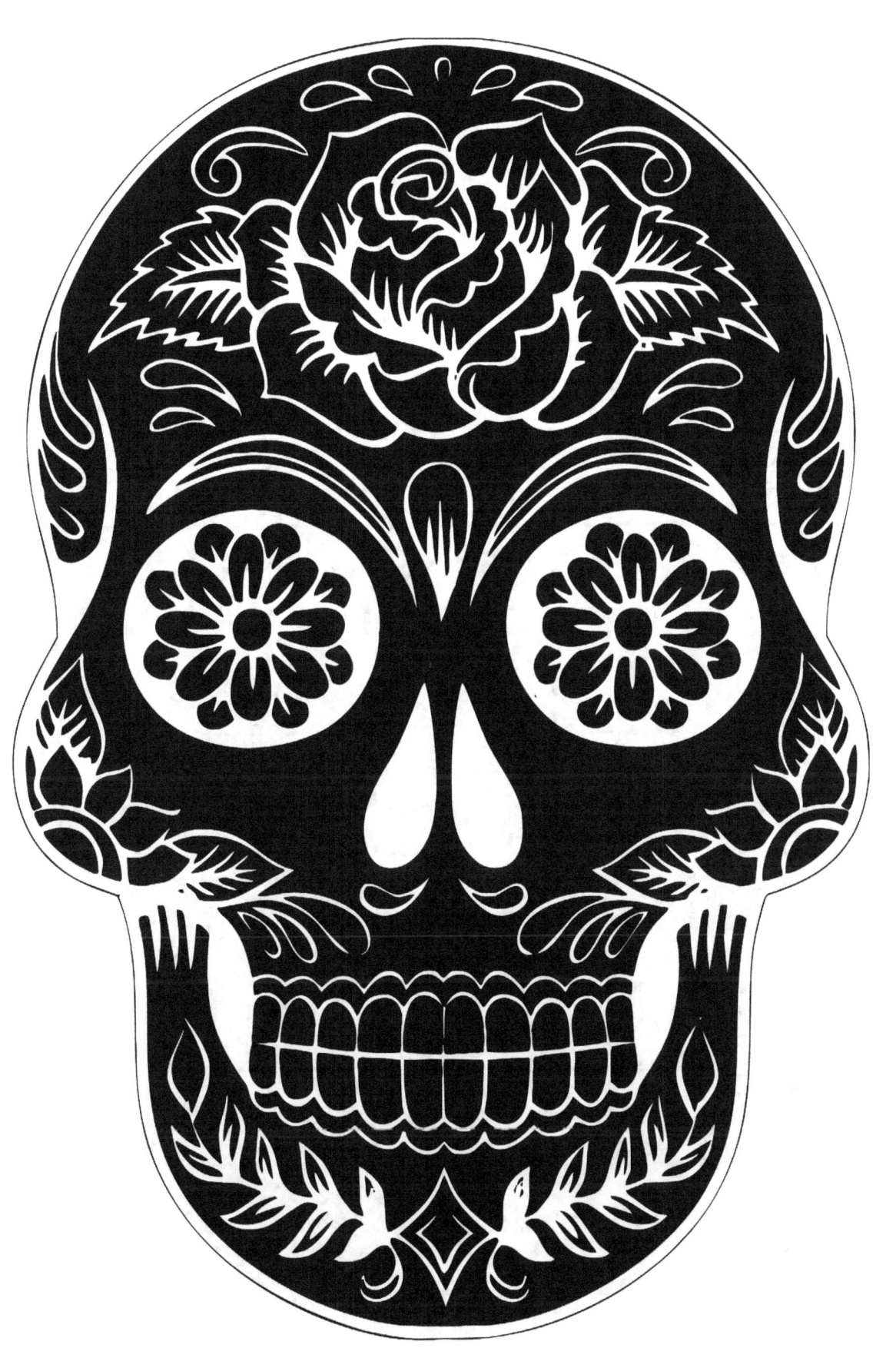

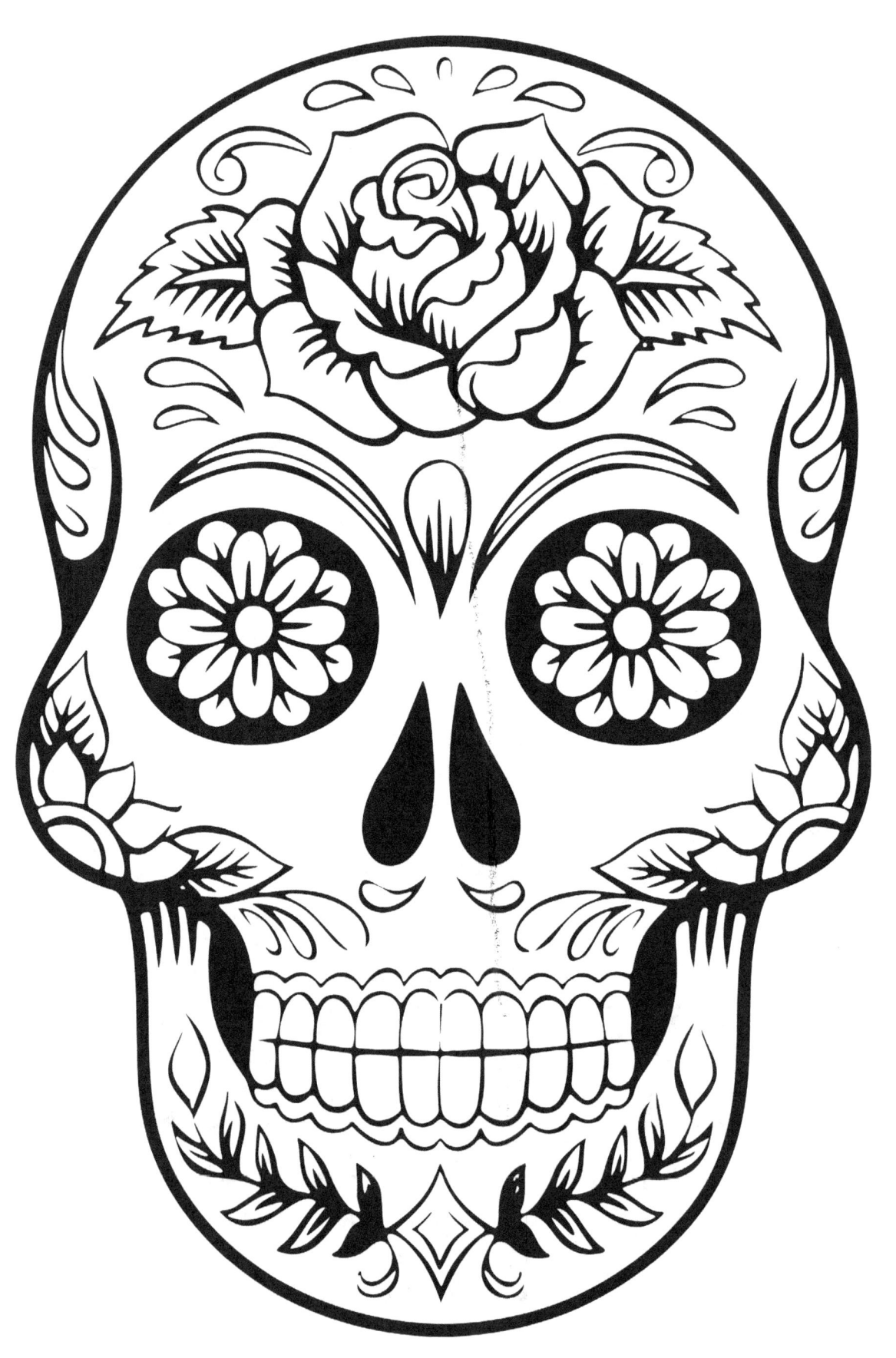

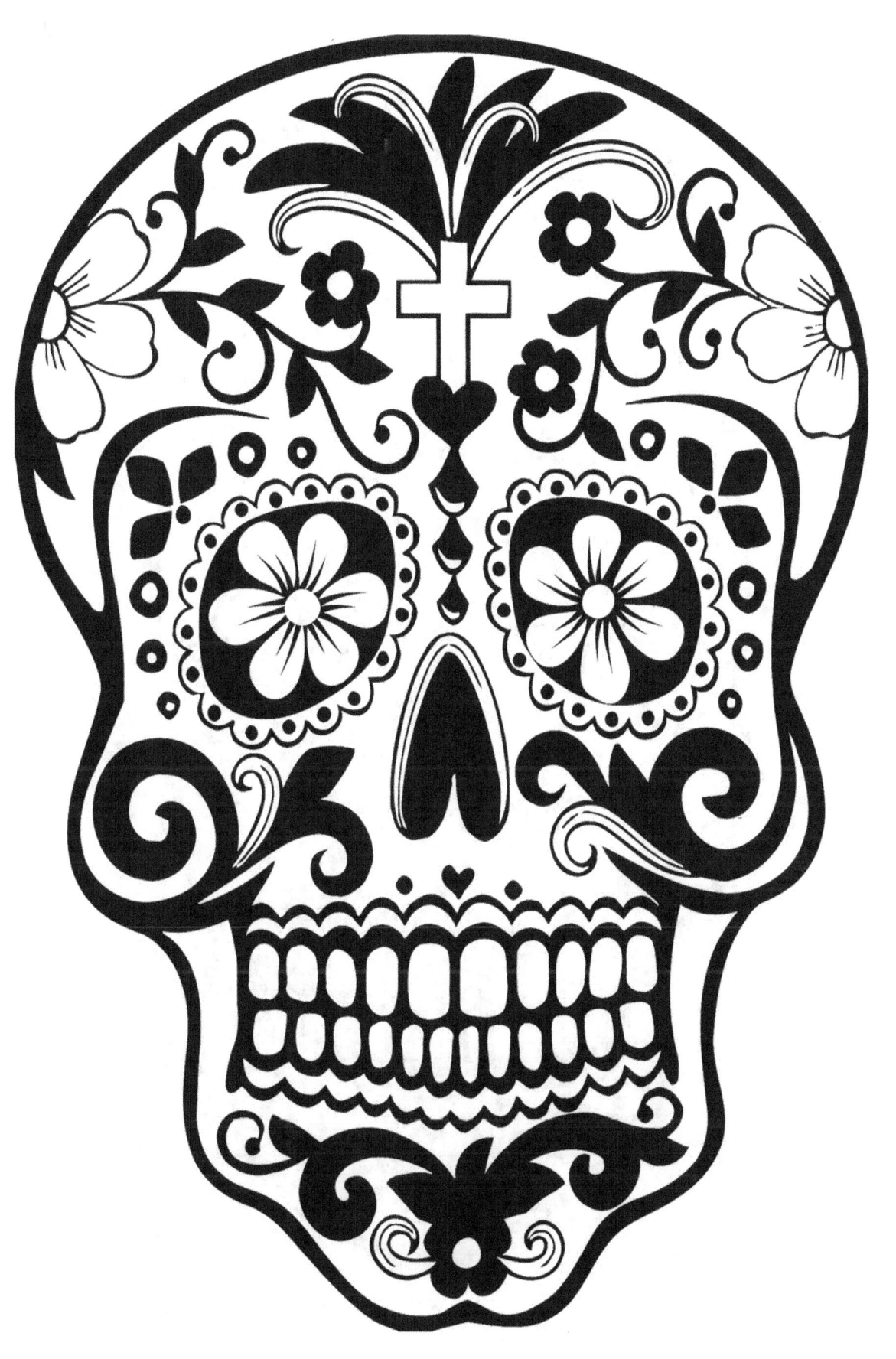

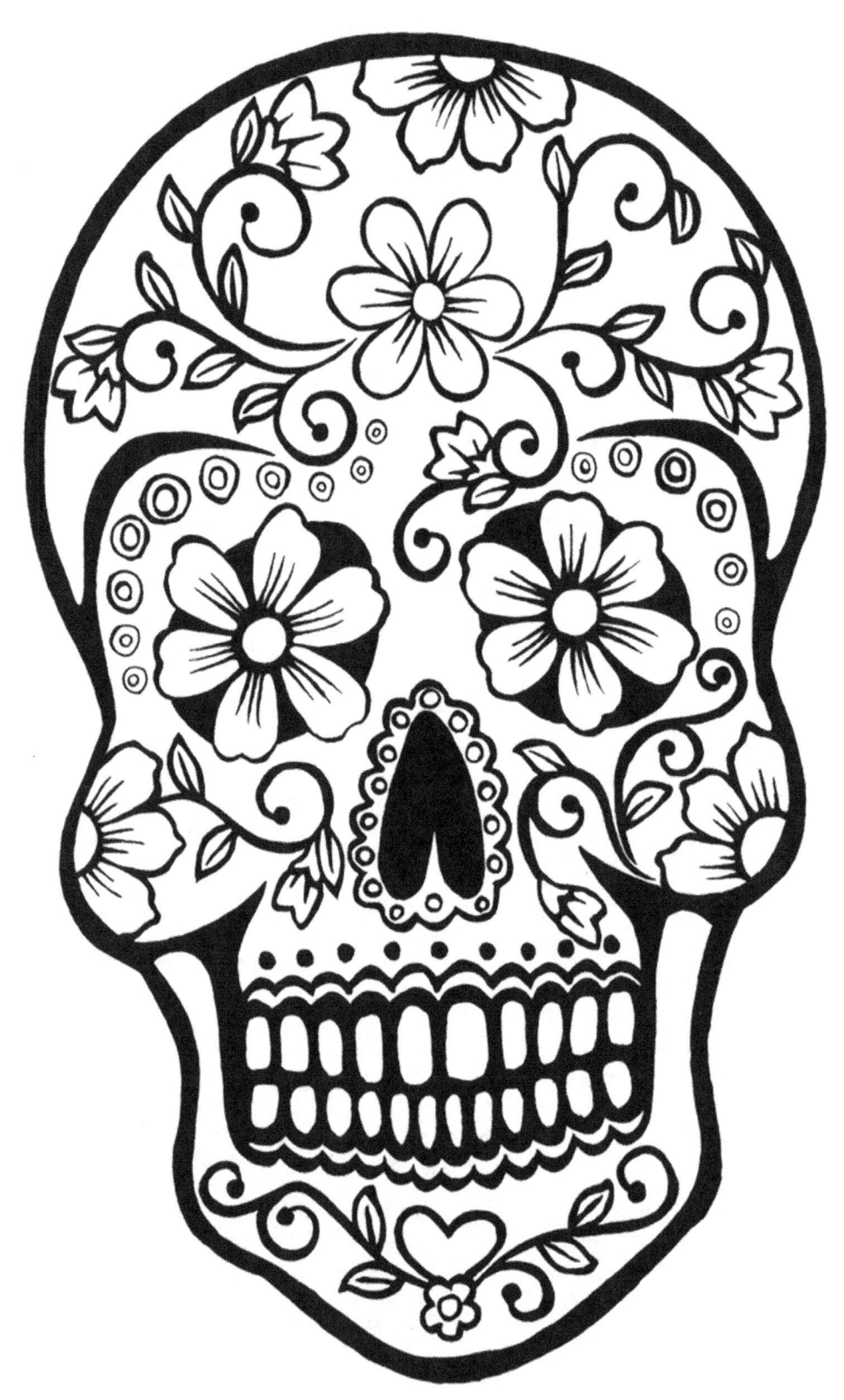

PESCNO.BLOGSPOT.COM

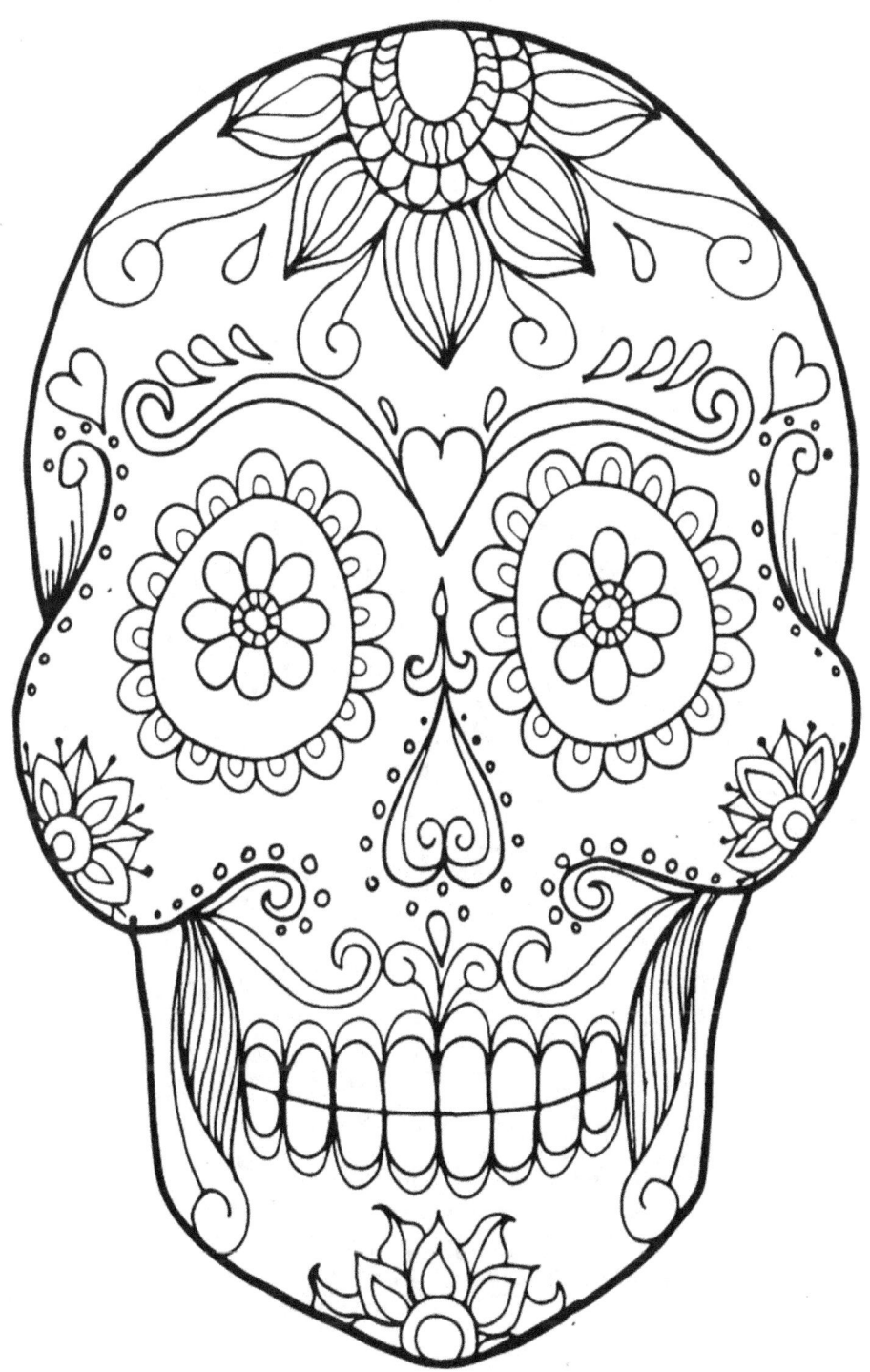

Copyright © 2015 by Monika Mira

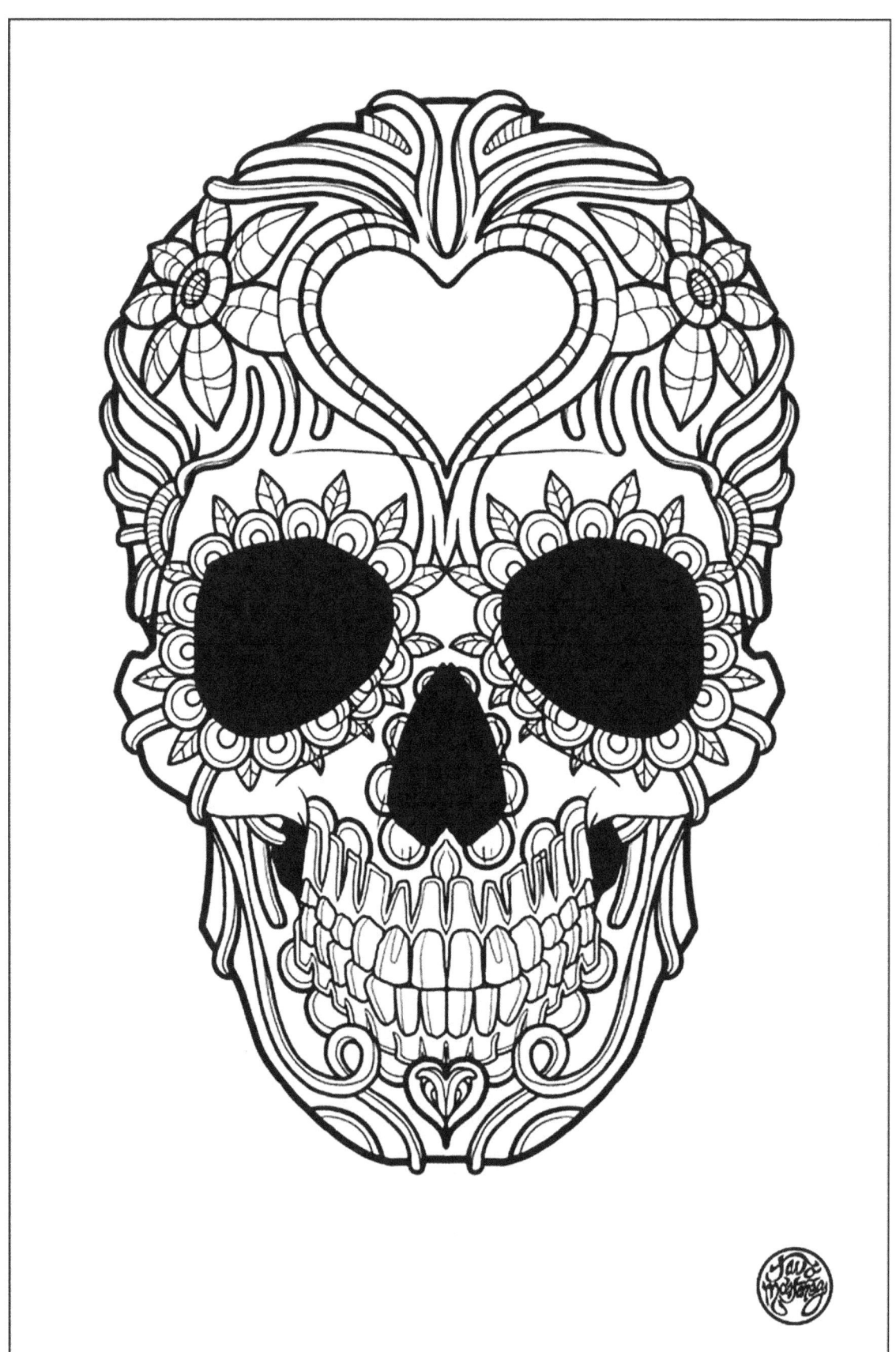

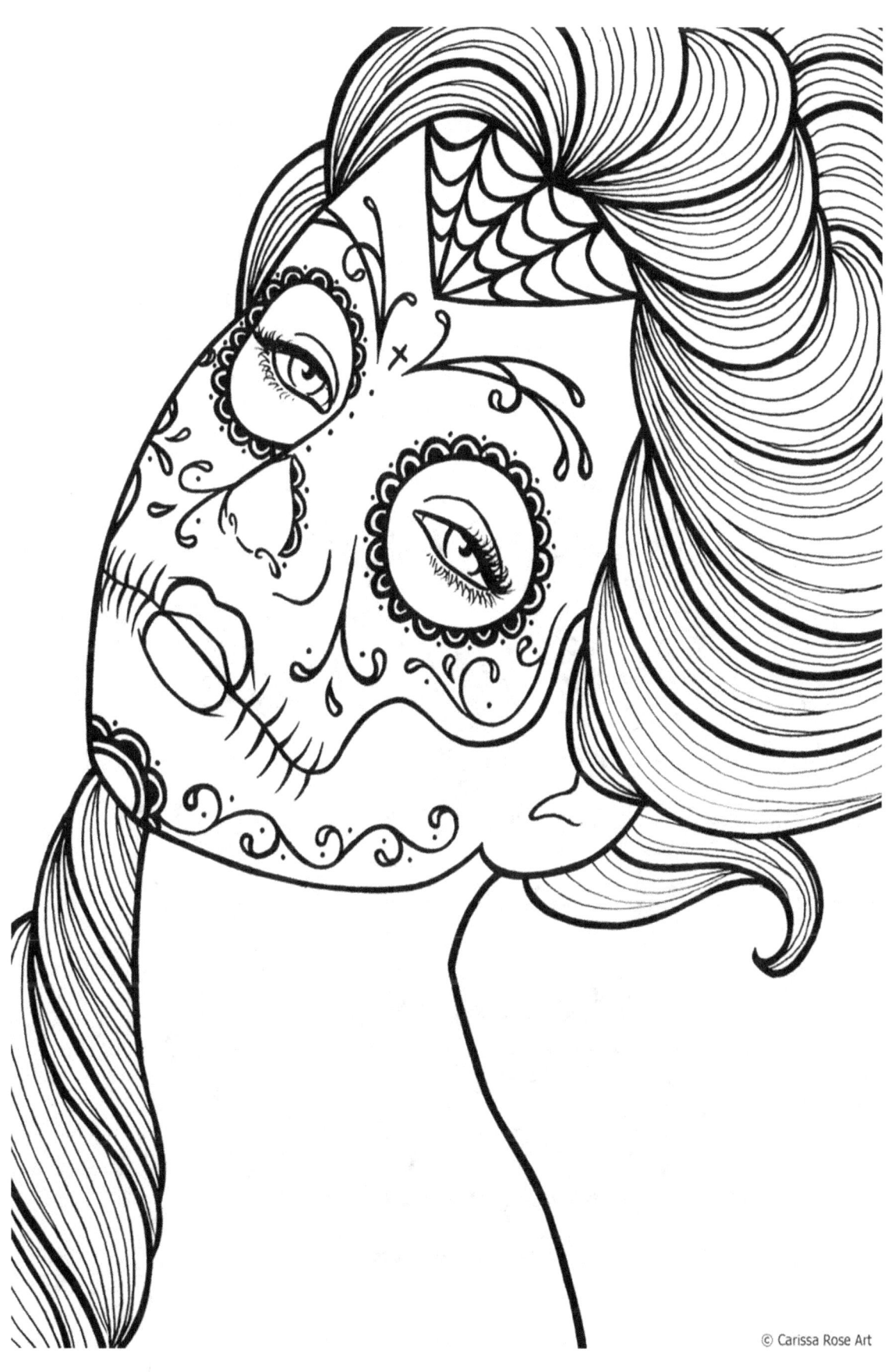

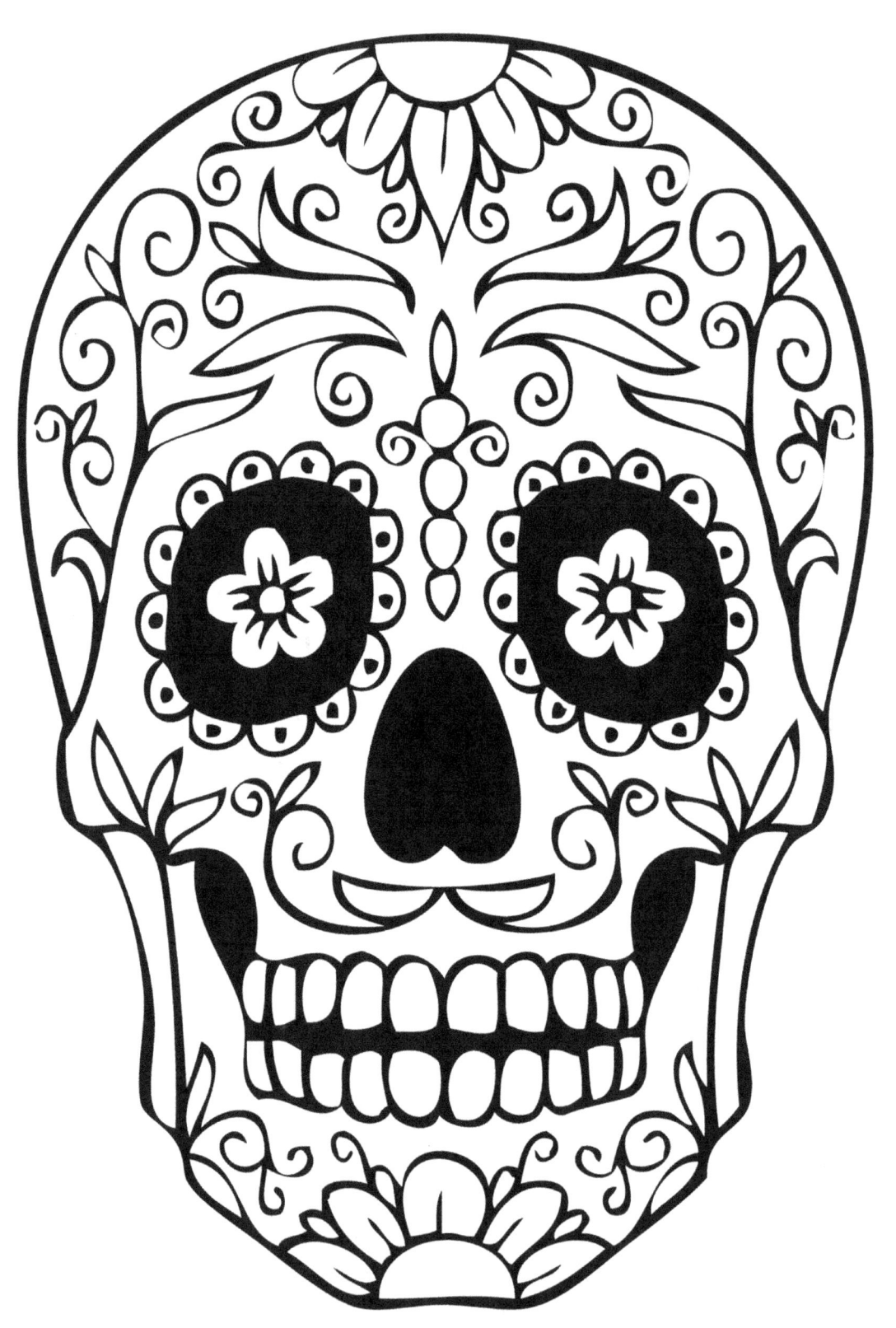

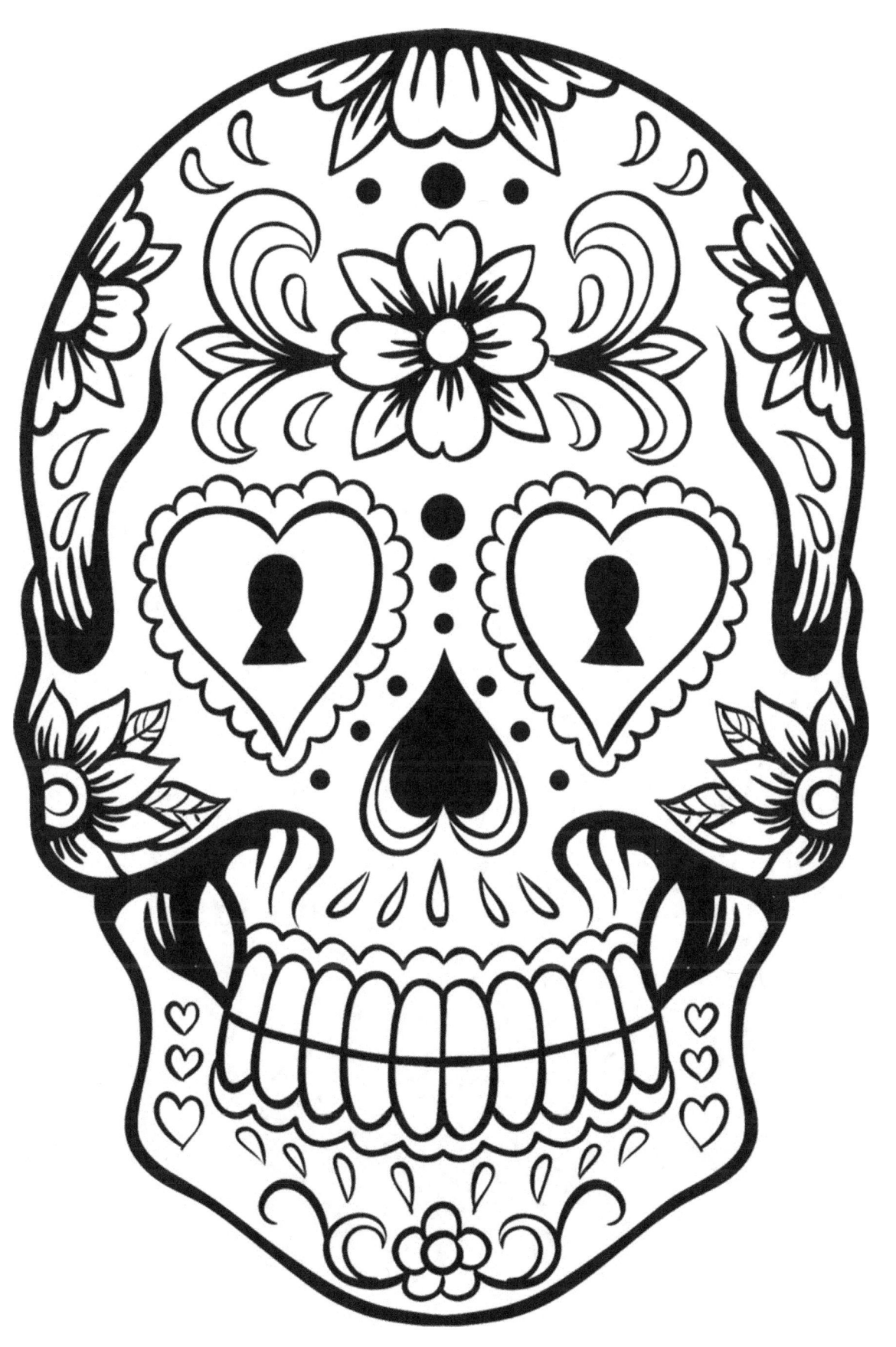

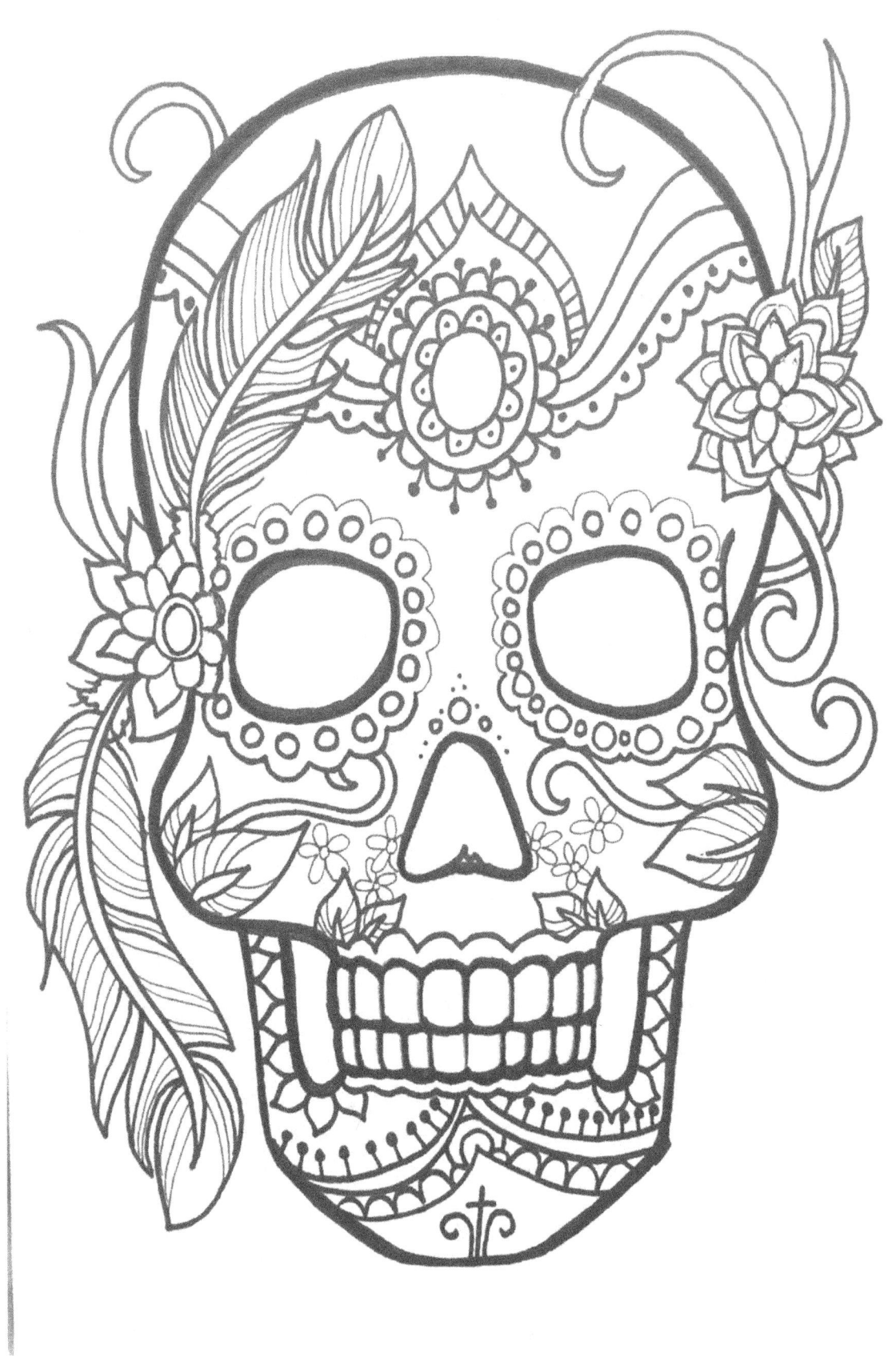

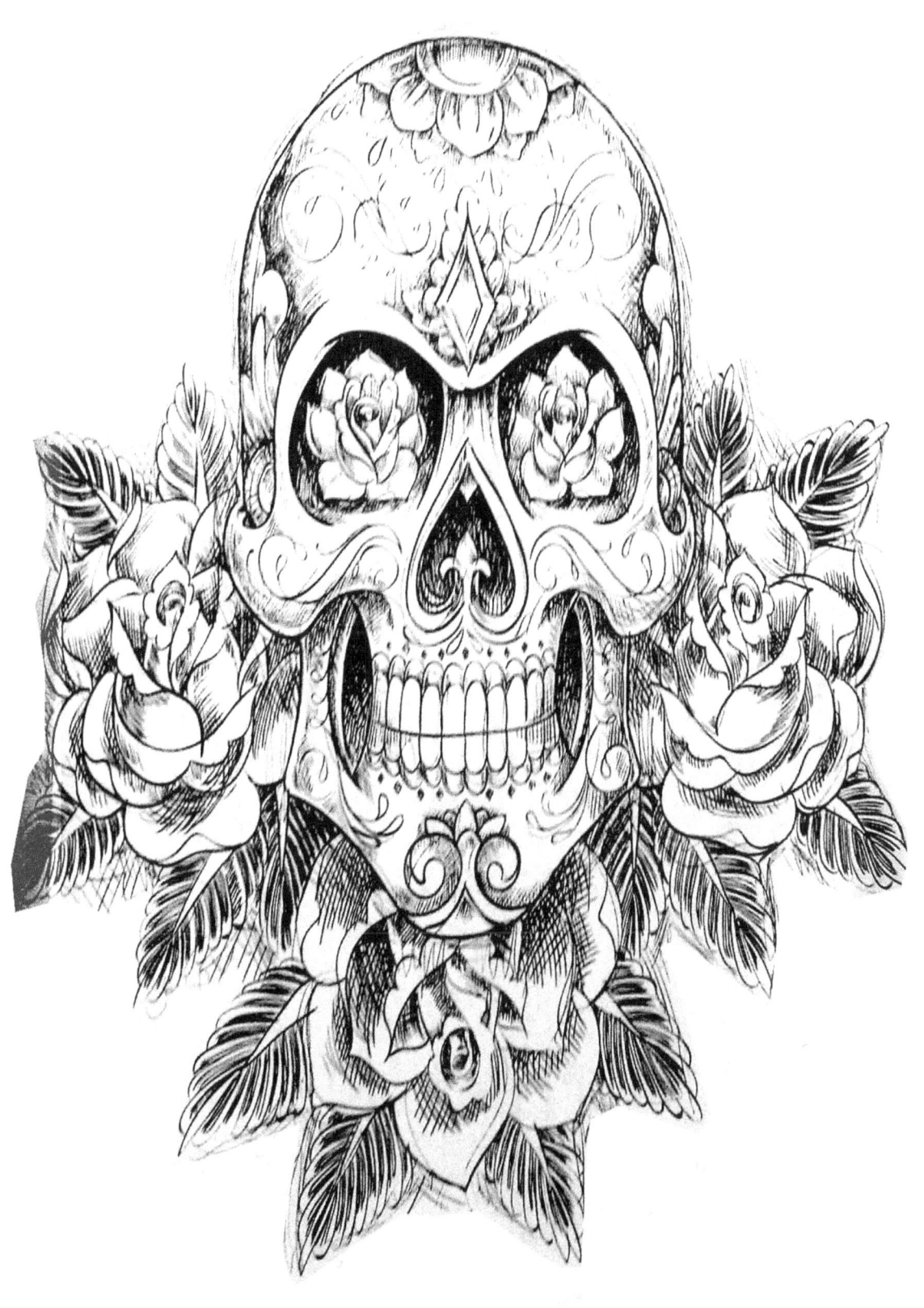

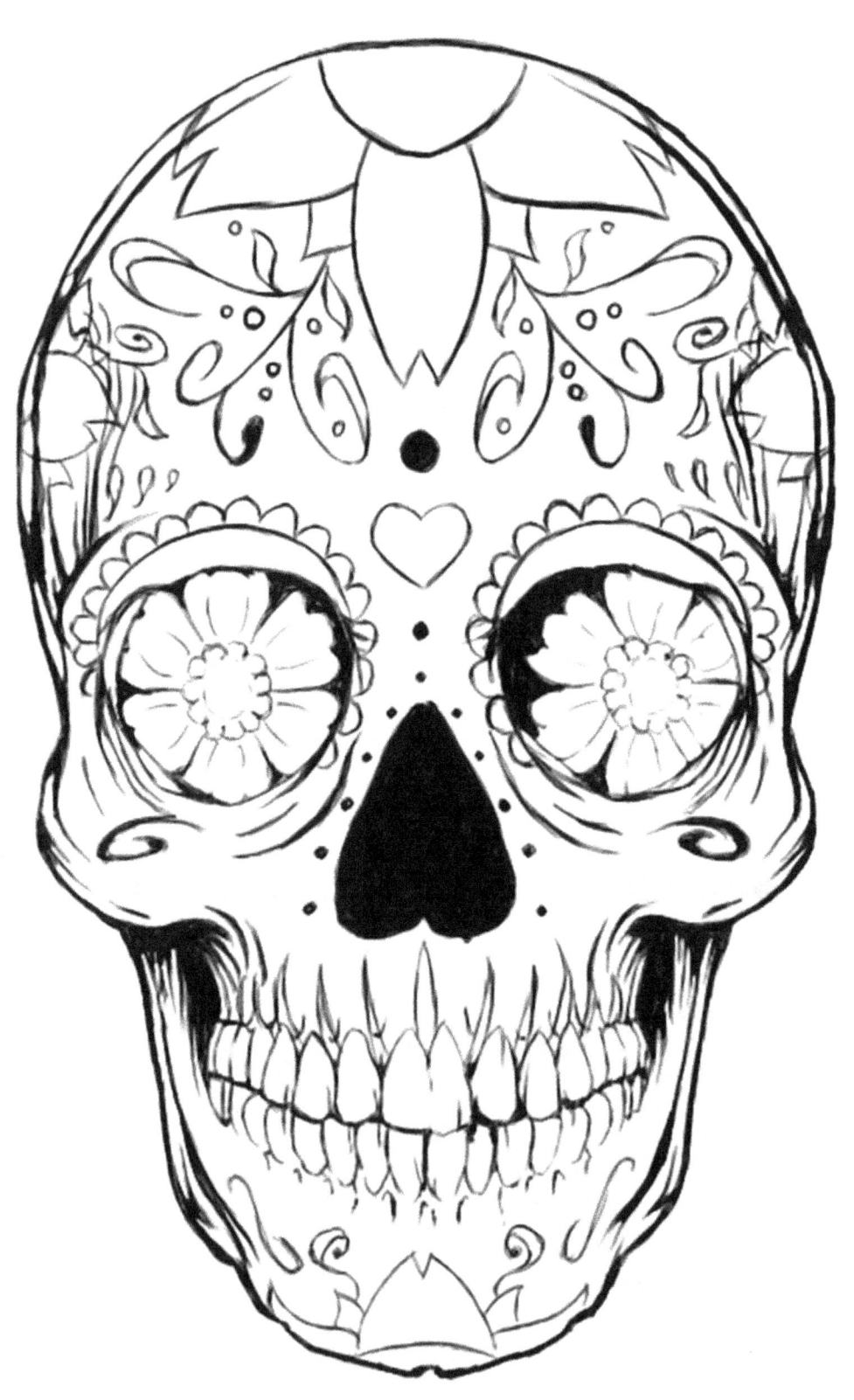

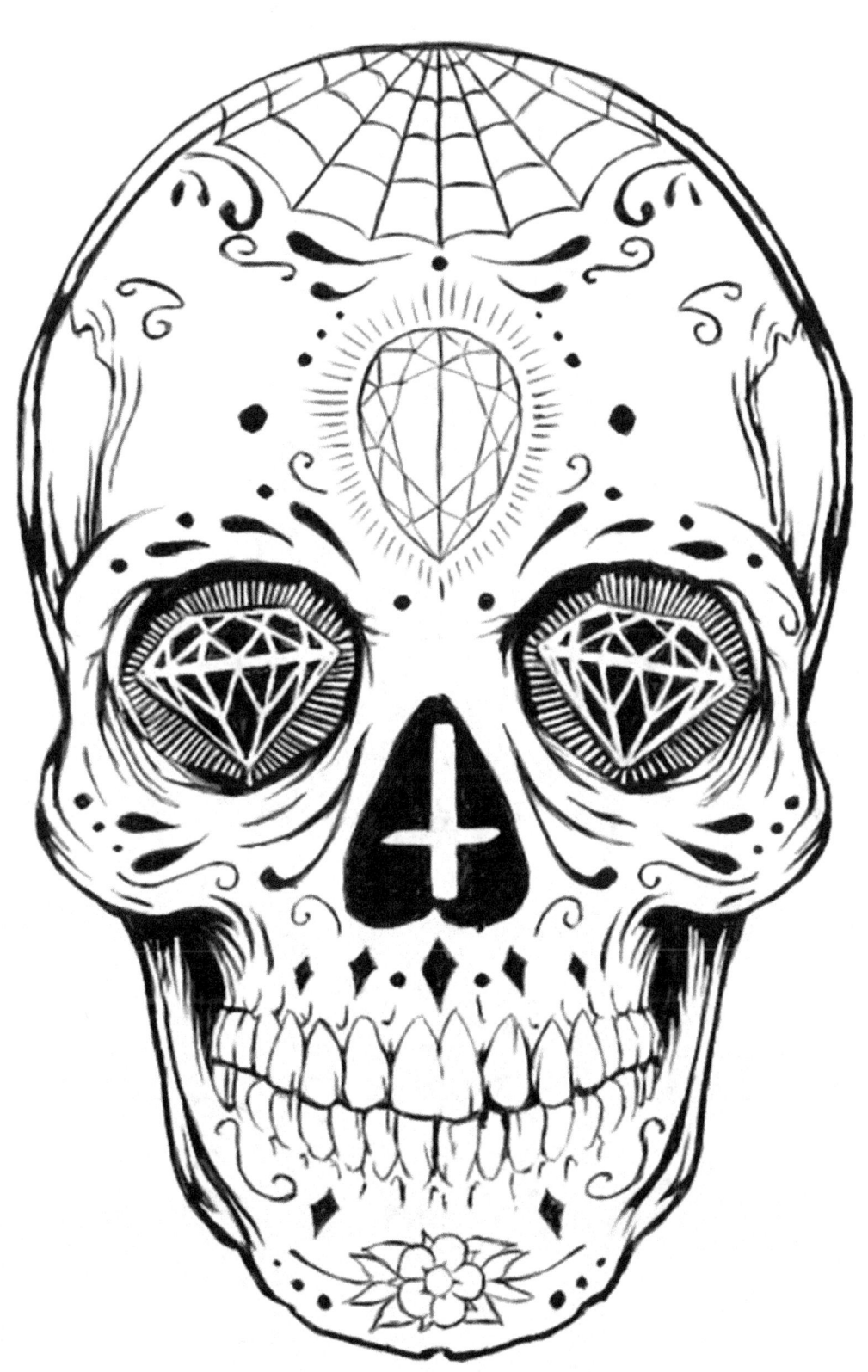

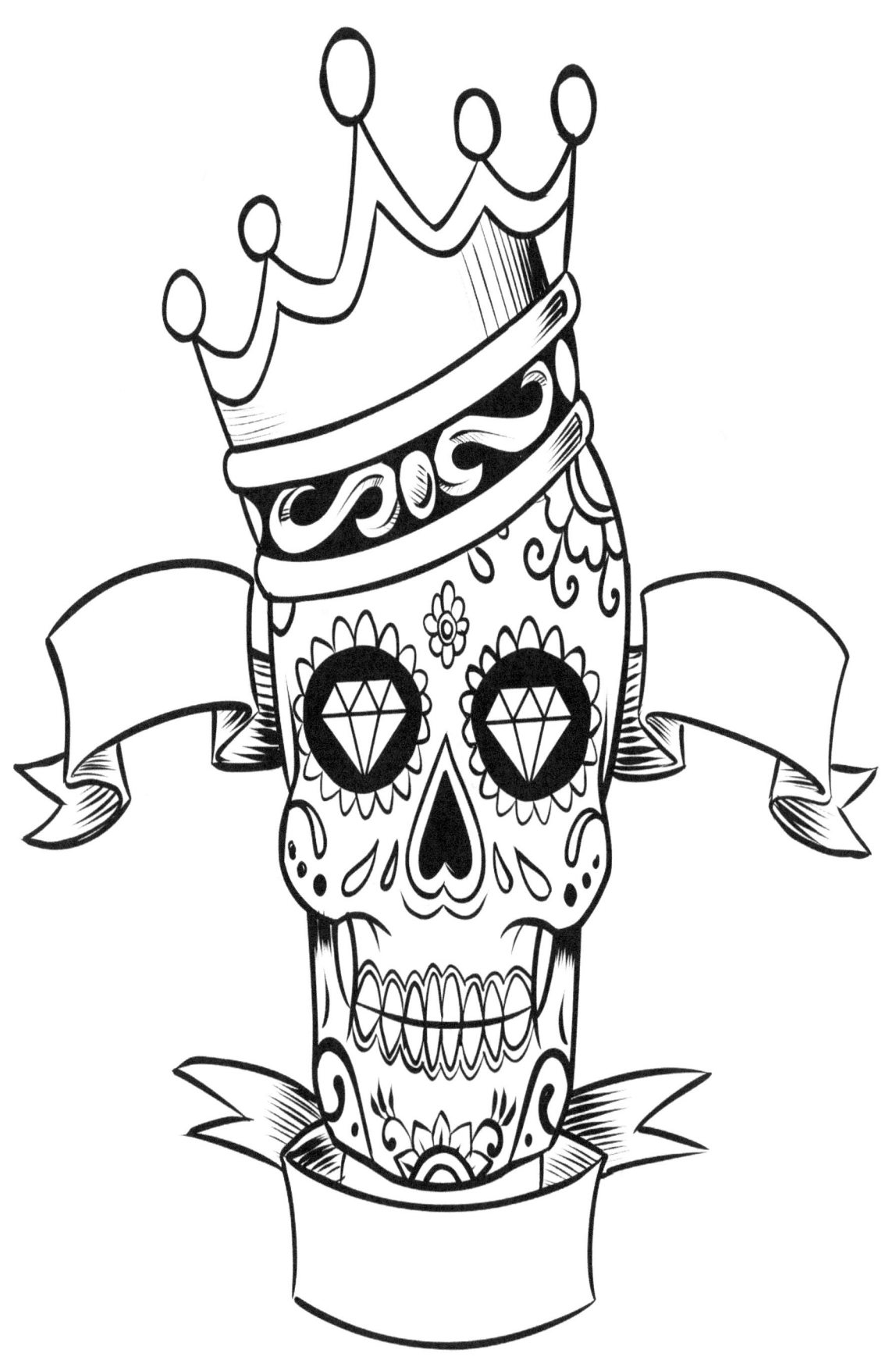

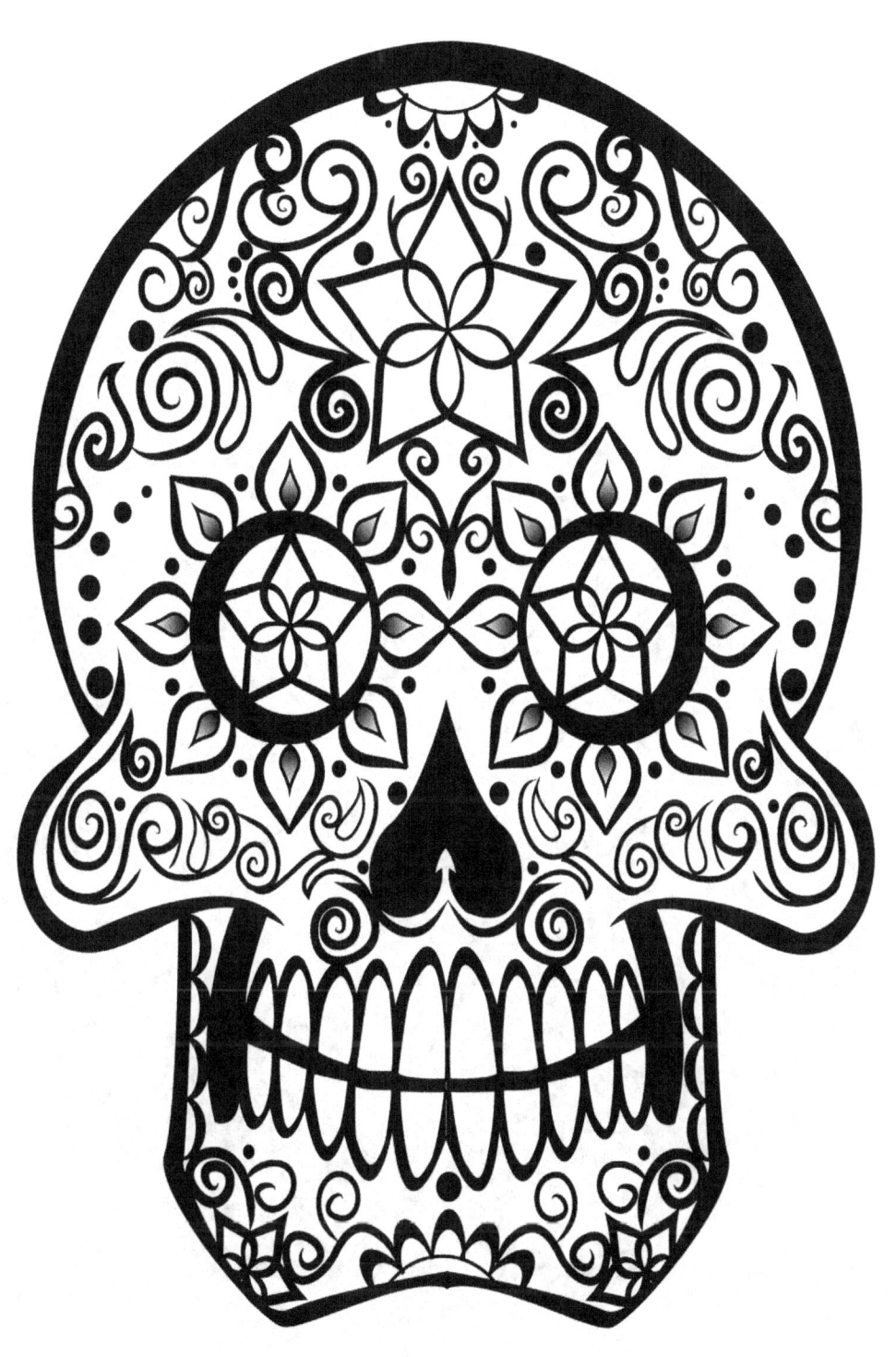

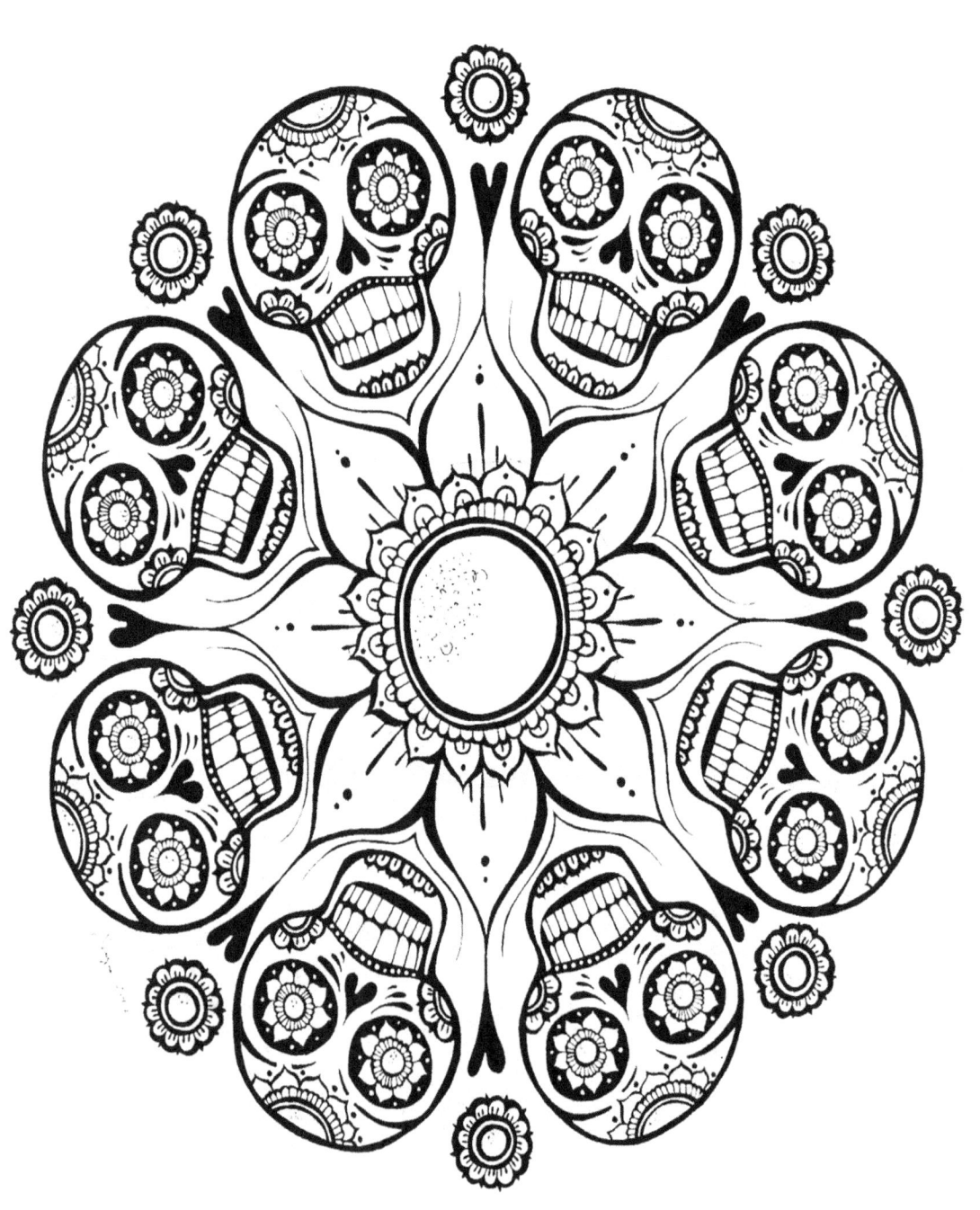

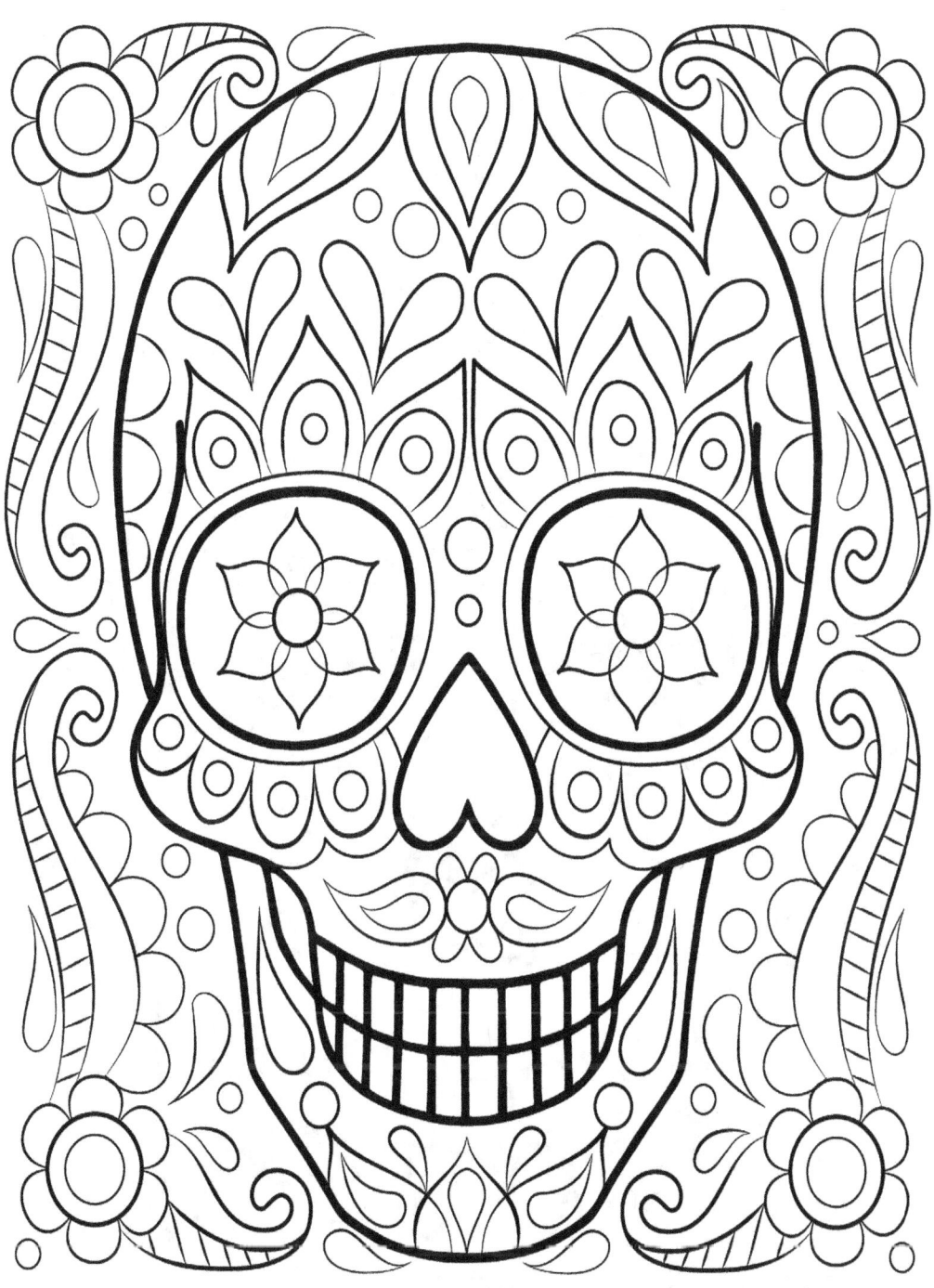

From "2016 Posh Coloring Calendar" - www.art-is-fun.com/coloring-calendar

Check out my Sugar Skull Coloring Pages ebook - www.art-is-fun.com/sugar-skull-coloring-pages

© Thaneeya McArdle • All Rights Reserved. For Personal Use Only.

www.thaneeya.com • www.art-is-fun.com

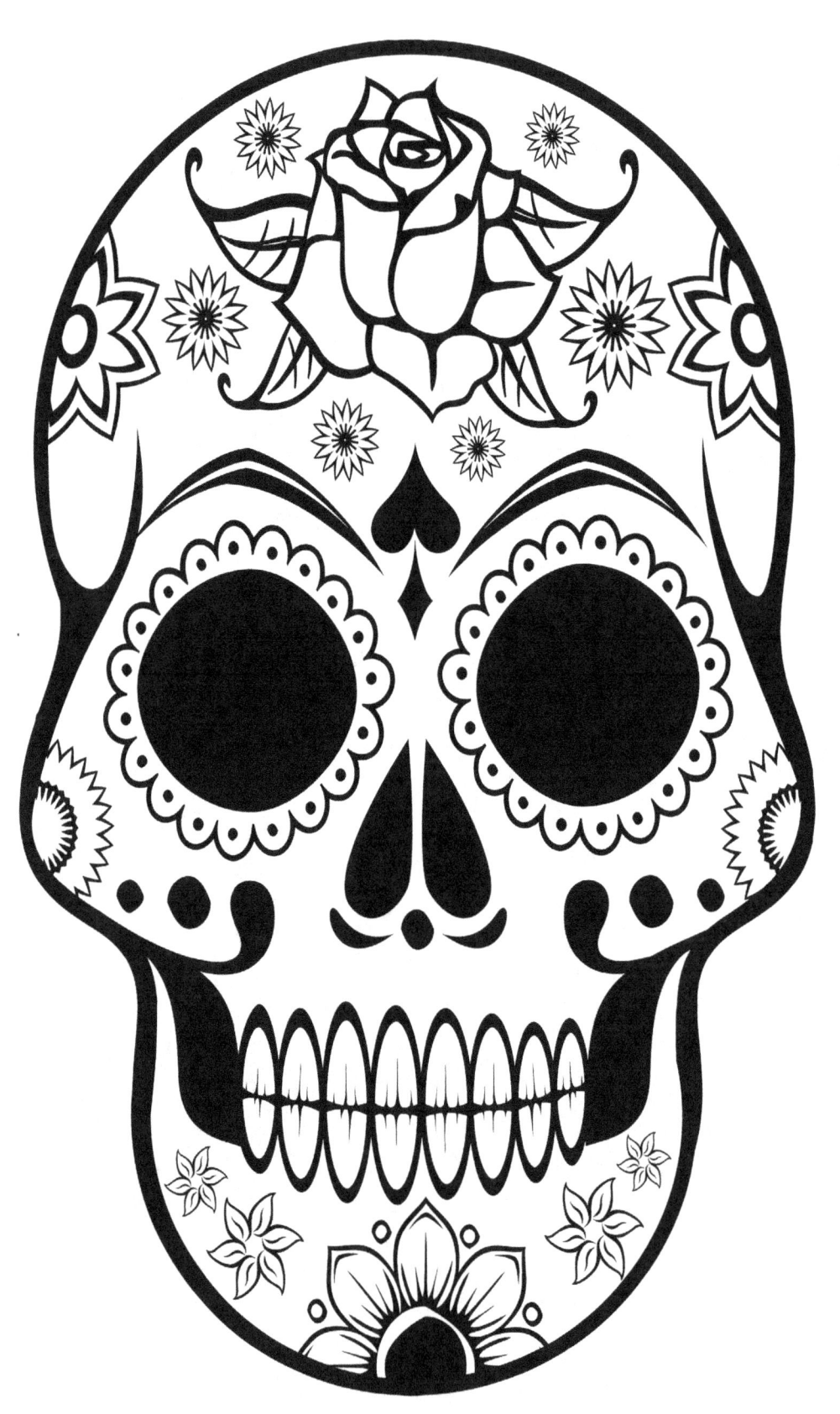

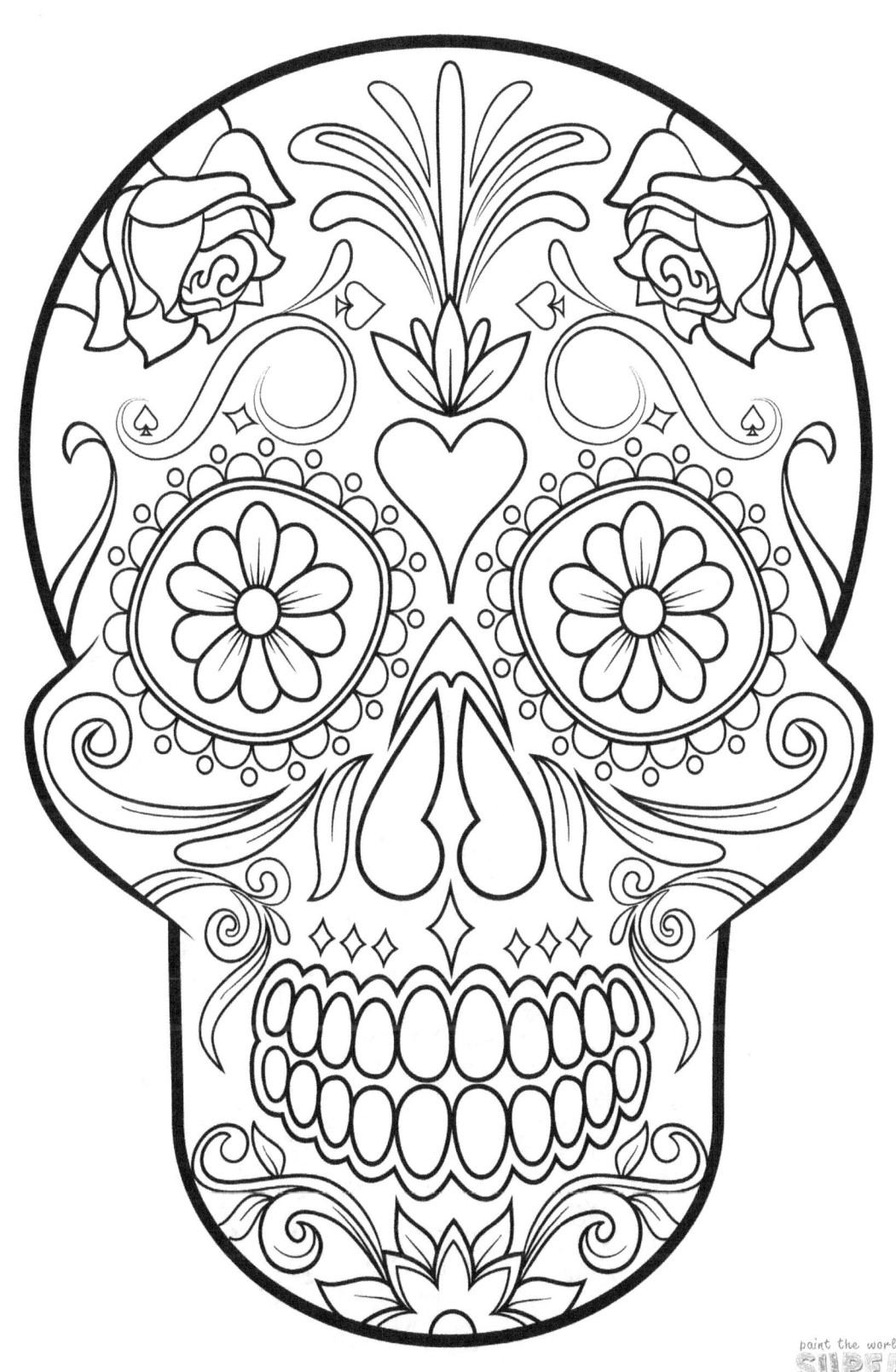

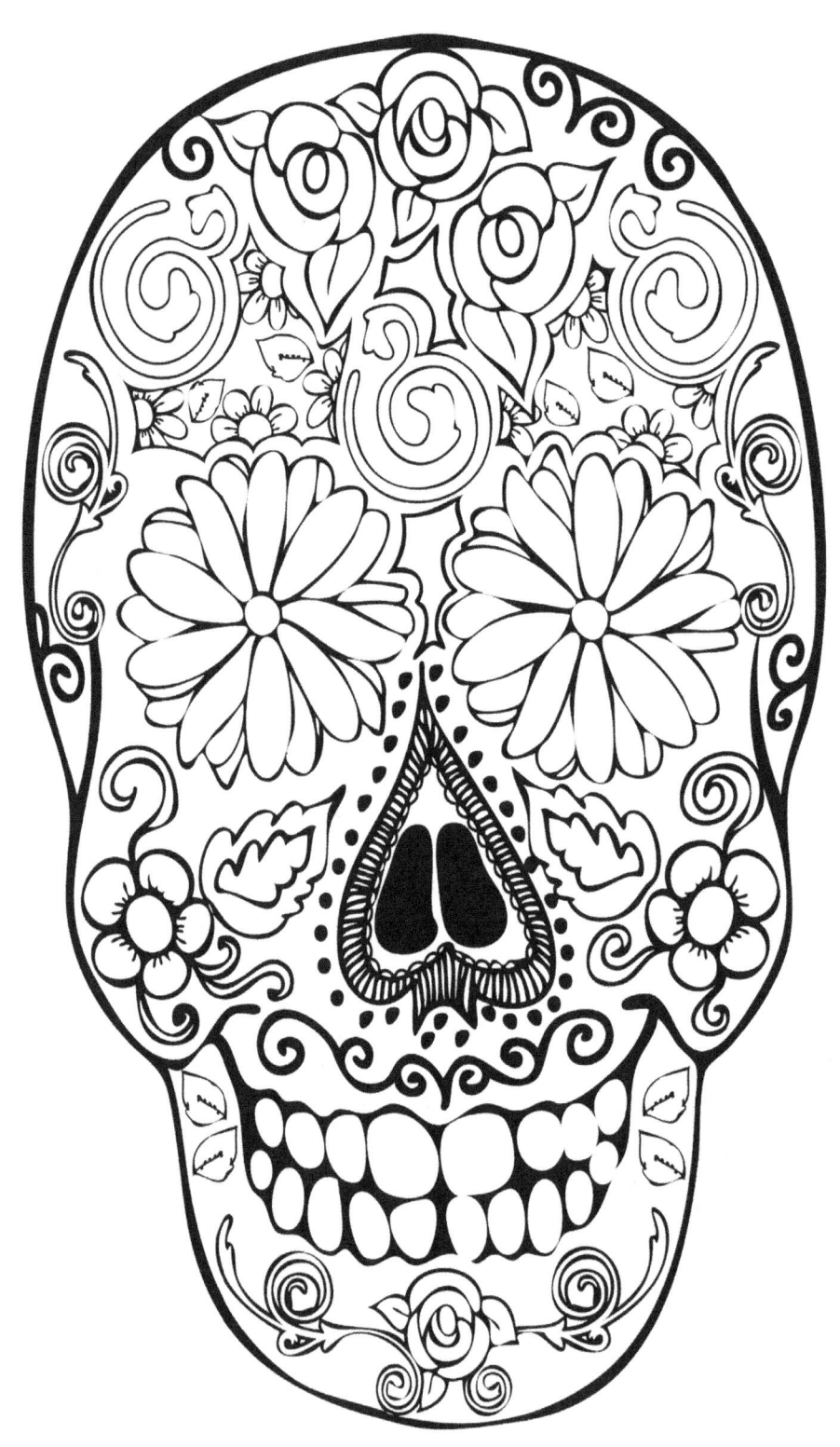

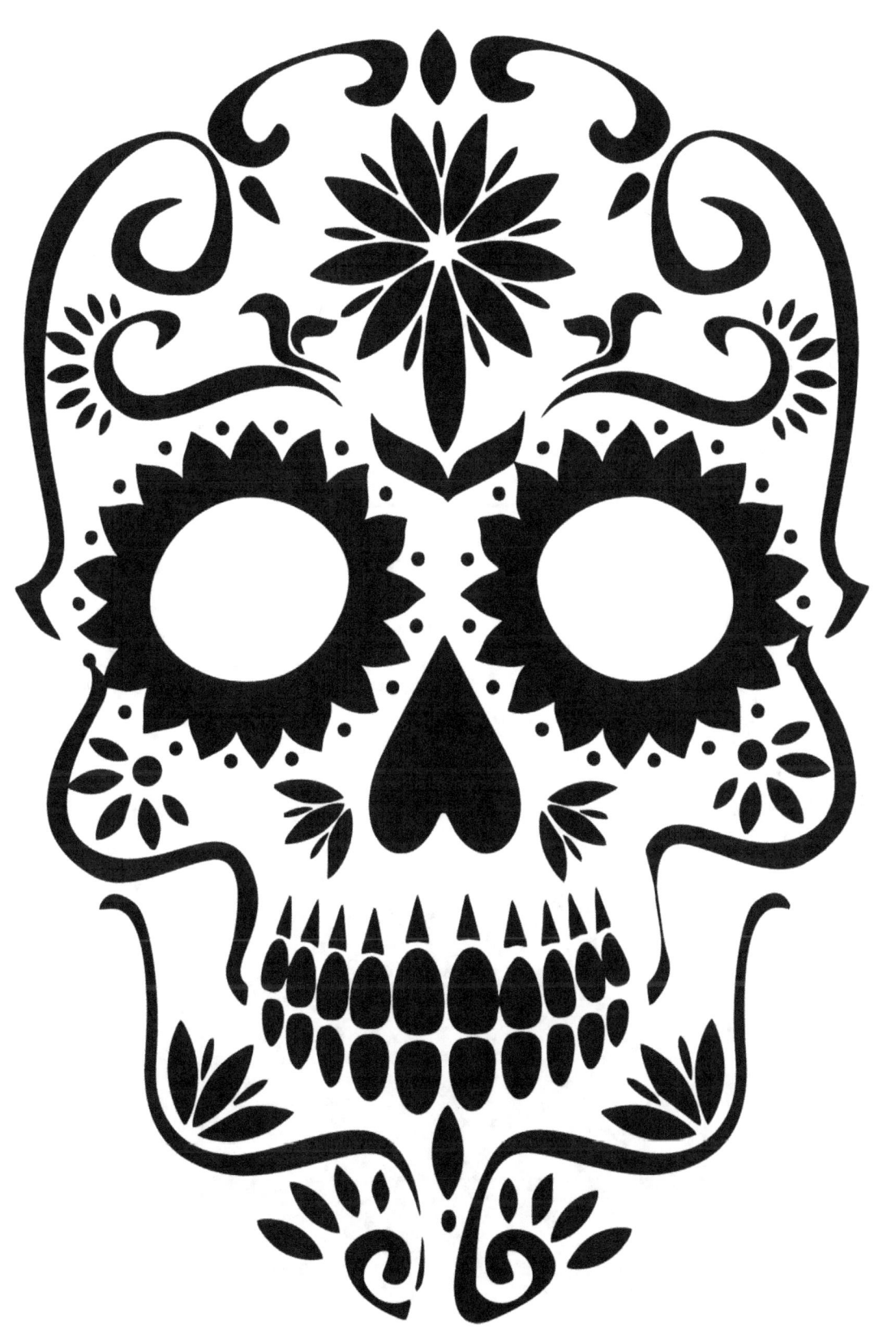

www.ingramcontent.com/pod-product-compliance
Lightning Source LLC
Chambersburg PA
CBHW062209220526
45470CB00009B/2987